THE GRIT

THE ONLY THING YOU NEED TO MAKE MILLIONS

BY MATT MANERO

THE GRIT
BY MATT MANERO

TABLE OF CONTENTS

1
WHAT IS "GRIT"?

I built my businesses from the ground up—I can tell you everything about struggle, sacrifice, and determination. I can also talk to you about finance, team-building, and investing smart. But there is one thing that towers above all else as the key to success: **Grit.** Grit is the *only* reason that my businesses have survived and thrived for over 20 years.

Grit is the ability to do anything legal to make it. **Anything.** Once you get clarity like that, it's game on. Grit is the determination to dig in deep, day in and day out, to achieve a meaningful benefit. It's not just seeing the goal, but muscling up the commitment to stay with it no matter what obstacles come your way, and doing it over and over and over for a long time.

I use the term "Grit" in this book as it relates to owning a small business, but it takes Grit to accomplish anything worthwhile in life. If it's easy, then it doesn't require Grit. Grit only kicks in when things start to get hard.

I'm talking insanely hard—much harder than you think. It doesn't take Grit to go to work when you are sick. It doesn't take Grit to hire someone because you no longer want to do that type of work in your business. It doesn't take Grit to make 10 cold calls per day. If you think these things take grit, you need to **wake up.**

You need Grit when: your cash is gone, your line of credit is maxed out, your last client is taking bids from competitors, and you lie awake in bed, in a cold sweat, terrified of how you are going to make payroll or pay the mortgage this month. You refuse to talk about it with anyone because you feel like a failure. You are alone in this battle against the failure of your business.

You need Grit to: Get up. Instead of going back to sleep, get your ass out of bed at 3 a.m., shower, dress like a pro, and get to the office while it's still dark out. You need it to start making 150 cold calls a day to save your business, instead of sitting there and wallowing in your misery. And you need Grit to do this day after day, week after week, until the tide turns in your favor again.

Could you do this? Have you ever done this? Ask yourself, have you really ever pushed yourself to a level of Grit that made a massive difference? Or are you just watching the ship hit the

shore, paralyzed even though you know you are going to sink with it?

Grit is vital, but it isn't free. And it's definitely not pretty. Grit comes at a cost: a sacrifice, a level of commitment that most people just can't handle. Don't tell me about missing your kid's play or your date night with your wife to fill a customer order. That's entry-level Grit. When the tenth bank turns you down for a loan, Grit is what gets you to the eleventh bank. It's the thing that keeps you going one hour, one day, one week after other people would have given up. Grit shows up for you—when you show up for it.

Prove Your Grit

Can you dig deep enough to find your Grit? Or do you claim to have it, only to crumble at the first, second, or third punch in the gut? Do you give up when your business plan fails, or when your project falls through? Do you say you are pushing yourself, when deep down, you know you have more to give?

Or maybe even worse—you haven't failed much at all. Your business is actually OK. In fact, life is OK. The bills are getting paid, cash flow and revenue are decent, but deep down, what hurts is

that you know you never rolled the dice, and never risked enough to find out if you have the Grit to make it **BIG.**

Instead, you backed off; you settled. Now you are living on the scraps, the leftovers. These scraps might be acceptable levels of achievement for most, but below what you are truly capable of achieving. Real Grit in my book is having the balls to never live on leftovers: to push yourself to a level that makes others collapse; to endure the pain of constantly being uncomfortable so that you can one day, *maybe*, reach your goals and dreams.

The truth is you might have some in the tank, but you just haven't tapped into it. You have played it safe, and the Grit you have tested is "low-level Grit." You limped into your career or business, stayed small, and made a decent living for yourself and your family.

But that's not true Grit—not to me anyway. I'm talking about a lifestyle of Grit: **a thought and action process** that gives you the confidence to know that no matter what obstacle is in front of you, it will be conquered.

Commit to real Grit now. Not to the little bit of drive that puts you ahead of your parents' success, or your neighbors' success, or your friends' success. I'm talking about committing to Grit so deeply, that when negativity, adversity, bad luck or maybe even death stares you in the face, you say, "Bring it on, bitch."

Keep Showing Up

During my career, I have had money and I've been broke. But one thing remained constant: I kept showing up every day. No excuses, no reasons to put work on the back burner—just an unyielding drive to make my life and my businesses successful.

Since I started in 1995, **my companies have funded close to $1 billion in equipment loans and leases and with current fundings of over $100 million per year and growing.**

I should have quit many times along the road—just tossed in the towel and said enough is enough. I was often overwhelmed by the pain of being a small business owner. I

> **GRIT TIP**
>
> *Grit is a way of life. Don't go easy on your own Grittiness. Force yourself to operate at a level of Grit that makes others cringe.*

was often dealing with sleepless nights, a lack of communication with my wife and kids, and borrowing from Peter to pay Paul.

But I didn't quit—that's where the Grit kicks in.

The sad truth is that most owners live in the "pain" and struggle side of business forever. The data tells us that **50% of small businesses fail in the first year and 90% fail by year five.** Why are the numbers so bad? Why do so many fail? Many blame the economy, the government, lack of capital, or a myriad of other external excuses.

But for me, it's easy: The reason most businesses fail is because their owners don't have enough "Grit"— enough guts—to stay the course and get to the "pleasure" or success side of their small business. It's sad because most of us never create the businesses we dreamed of.

Without Grit, you will not reach the pleasure side of small business, you will stay stuck in the pain side.

You will always have things you don't want to do, but you do them anyway—to make a living and provide for your family. **GET OVER IT**. To me, it's that simple. The Grit lies in the limited group of business owners, who, despite the obstacles, and the pain, stay the course long enough to get to the pleasure side.

It's time to stop being a slave to your small business—trapped in an endless loop of pain, problems, and aggravation. Because

when your business gives you what it was intended to give you, you have reached the pleasurable side: **success.**

That's my goal: to help you get to the pleasure side of running your business, through Grit. Use this book to trigger new ways to ignite your Grit again. Write in the margins or at the bottom of the pages. Take these ideas, put them into place, learn to use the term "the Grit" in your office and your life. Get on board the Grit movement. **Now, let's get started.**

2
BUILD UP A GRITTY SELF ESTEEM

If you are going to move into a new level of Grit in your business, and your life, you are going to need to understand this simple truth: **the questions you ask yourself, and the thoughts you think, will determine how much Grit you have**.

The concept of changing your thinking should be easy, but it is poorly executed by millions of people daily. The result is a life lived with a lack of real Grit, a lack of self esteem and a lack of success.

If you think that you are not worthy of success, you will have a hard time finding the Grit required to get through the toughest times. In order to *be worthy* of achieving your dreams, you must **believe** that you are worthy of achieving your dreams. Training yourself to have high self-esteem will make all the difference in your thought and action process.

Your brain is your own powerful supercomputer, designed to deliver responses that will benefit you and your survival. But the problem is that we overload our subconscious with negative thoughts and fears, prompting automatic negative responses from our brains. Our brains have been trained incorrectly.

In order to get Gritty, you need to retrain your brain to think empowering thoughts in every situation, rather than negative, fearful ones. Commit today to learn how to use thoughts to improve your self-esteem and automatically strengthen your Grit.

Train Your Brain to Think Gritty

You need to stop allowing yourself to think negative thoughts so you can stop the destructive behavior that follows negative thoughts. Starting today, I want you to replace thoughts that lack Grit with determined, Gritty thoughts. Here are some examples of how to make the adjustment in your thinking:

Question #1: Is it time to grow our business and take on more orders?

Non Gritty Answer: We don't have a credit line big enough to fill more orders even we had them. Let's not go after more customers yet.

Gritty Answer: My company is the best company on the earth. I was ready for the business then, now, and in the future. I will do ANYTHING on the planet to earn more business and customers.

Question #2: Can we actually land a monster client?

Non Gritty Answer: That customer is too big for us.

Gritty Answer: That customer would be a complete idiot to not want to do business with me and my company.

Question #3: Can I handle this timeline?

Non Gritty Answer: Our staff is not up to the challenge to pull that off.

Gritty Answer: I can trust my team. They will run through fire for me, and if they don't, I will hire a team who will.

Question #4: Should we really spend the money to expand?

Non Gritty Answer: We can't afford that.

Gritty Answer: Nothing will stand in the way of me and my success. Especially not money.

Fight Your Bullies On and Off the Playground

You need to learn to build yourself up with positive self-esteem, or you won't get anywhere. I suffered from self-esteem issues for most of my early life. Self-esteem is fragile, and it's toyed with by many when we are young. Teachers, coaches, friends and even parents can intentionally or unintentionally affect our self-esteem, which can in turn cause deeply ingrained issues that take a long time to overcome. Our brain records it all.

The key is to understand how to overcome low self esteem, and to turn your issues into reasons to connect to your Grit.

Take me, for example. I was a fat kid. I was always both taller and heavier than the other kids my age. It was easy for kids to put "Fat" in front of my name. I dealt with being called "Fat Matt" daily during my early years at school—at the bus stop, inside the classroom, and on the playground at recess.

It was no wonder I hated going to school. I hated leaving the house most days. I knew what was coming: the skinny wise-ass kids on one side of the playground and Fat Matt on the other—hearing them tease, ridicule and torment me. It wasn't fun then, and it's not fun for me to remember today. **But it's important.**

While I was getting blasted for my genetics, in the cruel way especially reserved for young kids, **I was also being taught. I was learning about anger, fear, despair and most importantly, Grit.** I learned, at a very early age, the ability to deal with pain and fear through changing my thoughts **and my actions.**

I stopped my torment by taking action in the fourth grade. During another typical recess, I was the last one to reach the playground. The other kids were already there, ready and waiting. But this time, a sixth grader joined in. He was bigger than the fourth graders that normally put me through the paces, and coming at me with more hate and venom than usual.

Something clicked in me. I couldn't take another minute of it, not another second. It was now or never. If I didn't finally stand up for myself at that very minute, I knew I would regret it for the rest of my life.

The sixth grader and I squared off and fought. It was the first fight of my life, and I got my ass kicked. Despite my size, I didn't have a clue how to fight—I just knew it was fight or die trying. Each punch I threw came from my heart against the pain that I had endured. **I got my ass beat for thirty minutes straight.** Knocked down over and over by the sixth grader, but I just kept getting up

and coming towards him. I took such a beating that most of the kids stopped watching. The sixth grader was begging me to stop coming back for more, but I did not give up until the bell rang and it was over.

I remember dropping to my knees on the playground with a black eye, bloody nose and bloody lip, alone and sobbing. A teacher helped me up, walked me to the nurse's office, and called my mother to pick me up. I wasn't just crying because of the physical pain, but because of finally realizing that I had done what I had to do. I took control of my situation and was willing to die to change it. It was a watershed moment in my life.

The next morning, my mother begged me to stay home from school but I wouldn't. **She was protecting me from the embarrassment of the beating, but that was the wrong thought.**

I knew there was nothing to be embarrassed about, so I went to school. The kids at the bus stop were different to me the next day. They saw the fight, and some of them had been part of the bullying in the past, but today was different. We all knew it.

That day on the playground, fighting for my self-esteem, I found my Grit. I didn't know what it was called then, but since then I have fought my entire life to keep it. I had stood up for myself,

when no one else would, and that was the end of being called Fat Matt. I had proved to myself and to others, that I had the Grit to accomplish anything.

Build up your self-esteem any way you can. Push your confidence about yourself and your business to new heights, and when called upon, take enough action to create a change. Don't go easy on yourself or others. Ask yourself hard questions that fuel the greatness and confidence within yourself.

> **GRIT TIP**
>
> *The thoughts you think on a daily basis are triggers for the actions you need. Think Gritty thoughts in order to take powerful action.*

Focus on a constant flow of empowering thoughts, rather than weak thoughts, to help you retrain your brain to automatically fire off the answer you need need to move ahead— not the answer you need to stay down. Gritty thoughts are the fuel for Gritty actions, and action is the end goal.

3

COMMIT TO YOUR BUSINESS LIKE IT'S A MEMBER OF YOUR FAMILY

My wife and I have been blessed with three boys, ages 13, 10, and 9. They mean everything to us—we would do anything to support them, to ensure their success, and to help them reach their potential. If my son shows the slightest interest in guitar, I'm searching for used Fenders on Craigslist. If one of them wants to become a wide receiver, I'm throwing passes until my arm is ready to fall off.

The same goes for my business. I will do whatever it takes to support its ability to thrive. If I have an employee who is great at social media, I put them in charge of that. If someone shows a passion and gift for sales, I make sure they have a shot at making some. It's my job to ignite and maintain the hearth of my company. And just as my job is to be in the thick of things with my kids, and reprimand as well as praise them, it's my job to do the same for my business to push it to the next level.

And that's your job, too.

Commitment creates clarity. My role as the father of my children and the owner of my businesses is to lead with so much commitment to their success that I get the best they can offer. Regardless of the behavior or the results, I must walk side by side with them to bump and nudge them in the right direction. But I must never yield or give up on my commitment to them to guide, to assist, and to help. I can't sit back and bark out orders to them. Nor can I wait in the wings for them to make a mistake and pounce on them with "I told you so"s.

If you are going to move to a new level of Grit, you need to see your business as if it is a bonafide, full-fledged member of your family. Would you abandon your child if the going got tough? Of course not. And you shouldn't abandon your business either.

Fifty percent of all American businesses fail within the first 12 months, and 90% fail within the first 5 years. Is this going to be you? Only if you abandon your business by failing to get properly connected to your Grit.

You have to choose to change the outcome of your business, and your life. The goal is to get you and your business out of the pain side and into the pleasure side. Are you going to make it? Or are

you going to just be another loser, repeating the "I tried, but..." refrain?

It's easy to blame your business failure on external factors. You can cite reasons for failure ranging from lack of money and lack of connections to a poor economy. But the truth is that those are all excuses. Stop using them and believing them, and instead commit to your business regardless of the struggle.

> ## GRIT TIP
> *You would do anything for your children, and you should. Now put your business right up there with your children.*

To change this perspective, disallow excuses, and commit to a deeper level of Grit, you need to do one thing differently: Commit to your business like it's your child. Commit at levels so deep that you would do anything within your legal power to make it a success and not a failure.

Having Grit means that you are not looking for ways out, you are looking for every possible option, connection, and dollar to make it work. The reason a business doesn't make it is because the owners didn't commit to their business deeply enough, and don't stay the course long enough, to create long-term success. Most give up too early.

Staying in the Fight

By all reasonable standards, I should have given up on my business many times. I have been broke three times in my 20-year career. I was busted broke in 1995, when I started my business. I went broke again in 2001, and on paper I was broke again in 2008 during the Great Recession.

At times, I'm talking about "can't pay the rent" broke—in 1995 I was so broke that I once looked out my bedroom window only to see the repo man driving off with my car. Back then, my credit cards were maxed out, my bills came on pink pieces of paper, and whether or not I closed a deal determined whether or not I could buy food. My despair was weighing me down, urging me to give in and say those words: *"Well, I tried..."*

I was at my lowest point, living in my dumpy one-bedroom apartment with no money and no car. I was almost ready to quit. I felt like a complete failure. I called my only good client, Bobby Whitfield of Bobby Whitfield Trucking in Greenville, Texas. I told Bobby that my money was gone and I didn't know how much longer I could go on. I told him I was on the verge of saying, "Enough is enough."

But then Bobby said, in his deep Texas drawl, "You are my finance guy, and you aren't going anywhere. I'm going to buy another truck—you are going to finance it, and you are going to make it."

Bobby was much older than me, a born and bred Texas trucker. I was a young kid, down on my luck. I had no roadmap, but I(had a lot of desire and Grit, and Bobby recognized that in me. He believed in me at a time when I didn't even believe in myself. He committed to me like I was a member of *his* family, and gave me the confidence to recommit to my business, to dig in deeper than I thought possible and lay all my final cards on the table: to go for it or die trying.

Bobby's unyielding support of me and my business was a turning point that bolstered my Grit to stay in the ring and keep swinging. I dug in deeper than I thought possible, and made the true commitment to my business that Bobby's Grit and confidence enabled me to make.

I started working seven days a week. I spent Monday through Saturday cold-calling and visiting prospects (in a borrowed car), and Sunday driving around the city of Dallas looking for fleet vehicles parked for the weekend. I would write down the phone number, type of vehicle, color, and unit number, then go back to

my apartment and call their office to leave a voicemail letting them know that I would be calling them again on Monday morning to earn their business.

Hell, I would drive the highways of Dallas just to follow big rigs so that I could write the name and number of the trucking company down and call them, too.

I did anything and everything to find leads and people I could pitch. I had a sign made that read "TRUCK FINANCING HERE", and I mounted it to two pieces of wood that slid into the rear door-jambs of an old Chevy Suburban. I would put the sign up at truck stops in the early mornings and talk about truck financing to anyone who was willing to listen.

My in-the-trenches marketing allowed me to understand my industry at a level that my competitors couldn't fathom. It also helped me earn respect, win some new business and get really, really, Gritty.

Over the next few years, Bobby and I did dozens of financing deals, and we became close friends. My business turned around, and I started to thrive.

One day I received an early morning call from Bobby's wife. She told me that Bobby had been killed in a car accident the night

before. A young man, in the midst of an argument, had stormed out of the house without his shoes on, and ran across the road—directly into the path of Bobby's oncoming pick-up truck. Bobby swerved to avoid hitting the man, and his truck flipped over into a ditch. Bobby was killed instantly.

I was in shock when I heard the news. Then his wife told me his wish: she said that Bobby had always told her that if anything ever happened to him, that I was to be the first person she called and that, "I would make it right."

Bobby and I never talked about this, but when that task was put on my shoulders, I said, "No problem." I would make it right. I would repay Bobby for his belief in me when I needed it most, and for helping me to commit to my life and my business the way I needed to—with Grit.

Bobby's widow did not want to run his business, so we agreed that selling it was the best option. I worked hard to make sure she got good money for the deal. I packaged the company, marketed it to the industry, and sold it for $1,800,000 to a trucking company out of Kansas—not a massive sum of money, but enough to take care of her for a long time.

Bobby was there for me at a time when I needed him; he gave me the push to dig and connect to my Grit. Because of Bobby, I decided that my lousy financial situation was temporary, and pushed through it.

When I was broke, I did whatever I had to do to keep the doors open, and kept showing up every day, day after day, week after week. Every day, I continued to bust my ass at levels most people can't or won't reach. The key is to stay in the fight all the time, broke or not broke, stay gritty.

I stayed in the fight. Just like Bobby told me to. Just like I would stay in the fight to help one of my children. **Just like you need to do.**

4

THINK BIG AND SET GRITTY GOALS

It took me and my team 18 years to build a company that funded $36,000,000 per year, and *it took us just 18 months to blast off and fund $100,000,000 per year.* So why did I waste so much time and so many years being too small? I didn't dream big enough from the beginning. You too must think BIG—Bigger than you originally thought.

Of course, for many years I was successful by most standards. But some days I would still come home frustrated with my slow progress, with the difficulty in increasing revenue and profits, and with my inability to give myself a raise.

My wife used to say to me, **"You are so much bigger than your business."** It made me crazy, because she was pointing out that even though I was doing well on the surface, my business wasn't all it could be.

And she was right—but it wasn't what I wanted to hear. And so her comments caused us many fights, and for me, many nights on the couch. As much as I didn't want to hear it at the time, she was

right. My sweet 5'2" fire-cracker redhead wife knew me to the core—and knew I was capable of more.

She didn't give me the pat on the back I was looking for from her. She knew I was bigger than my business. I was capable of accomplishing more. MUCH MORE. **And so are you.**

In my mind, I was already gritty. I was working long, hard hours. But that was the problem. I was only doing what *needed* to be done, and not seeing the bigger picture. My efforts weren't moving the needle of net worth. The truth is my business was dying the slow death that thousands of small businesses die from each year. Because of my small goals, I was dying with it.

I thought my mind was clear, but it was cloudy. Sales were increasing and tax returns showed that we were earning slightly more year over year. We lived better than most of my family. I was even doing better than my dad did at my age. I should have been be proud, right?

Not in the world of Grit. I needed to stop simply "keeping up" with others, **and so do you.**

The real question is: **What can you accomplish? What are you capable of? How much bigger can you grow your business? And yes, how much more money can you make?**

Dream It First

When I decided to dream big, I committed to do two things:

1) Build a $100,000,000 business.

2) Become successful enough to shut my wife up.

A whole new level of Grit was required. Once you start to dream big, you will realize that you need to reach a new level of Grit.

Stop reading now and take a minute to **DREAM BIG**. I want you to see yourself in a mansion overlooking the ocean. Dream about no longer flying coach, and dream about you and your family flying in a private jet. Dream about how many people you can help, and how much money and how many opportunities you can create for yourself **and others**. I'm talking monster dreams, crazy dreams, nutso dreams.

Why? Because when you allow yourself to dream big, it will trigger an emotional response. That's what you want to feel. That feeling is going to give you a **gut-level Grit check.**

Once you start this process of massive dreaming, your brain will fire off emotions to your body. If you love the way you feel when you dream big, you have a chance to actually reach those goals. If the thought of being that big scares the shit out of you, it might

not be right for you and that's OK too. You need to put yourself through the process of really dreaming big to test your Grit. But for some of us, when we allow ourselves to really dream big, we love the way it makes us feel. And then somehow, we find the wherewithal to muscle up the Grit to make it happen. If that's you, then congratulations, because you have just entered a new level of Grittiness.

> ### GRIT TIP
> *In order to tap into your Grit at the deepest level, you need to build **your life** by **your design**. Use the Grit Goal Wheel to design your life with your own goals and dreams.*

Create Your Own Roadmap

The problem with dreaming is that most don't do it enough. **We just go through the motions, day after day, with a roadmap that makes no sense.** The roadmap could have been created for us by parents, schooling, fear, or simply a lack of Grit. In other words, we might be living a life that doesn't represent what we want or what we are capable of achieving.

I might love doing business with a one-person cabinet maker, but he might hate being a one-person cabinet maker. He might want to be 100-person cabinet maker, but he never took the time to dream about it. He ends up frustrated, unhappy, and angry all the

time. He is stuck in the pain side of his business. Subconsciously wanting more, but never getting it. To him, and to you, goal setting is essential.

Set Your Goals Daily

I used to hate reading books that harped on the importance of goal setting. Why? Because I wasn't setting goals, so I rebuffed the idea. I don't look at goal setting that way anymore, because I have made it a daily habit. It's part of my Grit.

If you want big time success in business, you must set big time goals that cover all aspects of being bigger. Your goals must be big and specific. Your goals must address how many employees you want, how many people you can help, and what your annual revenue is going to be. And yes, you need to have goals of greater profits and a larger net worth.

One of my mentors, author of *The 10X Rule*, Grant Cardone, says it best: "If I set and review my goals twice a day for an entire year, that's 730 times per year. If you set your goals once a year on January 1st, who do you think has a better chance at reaching them?"

THE GRIT
BY MATT MANERO

Decide today what you want tomorrow. Write your goals down every day as a reminder to you to not waste time being small. Go BIGGER from the beginning.

The Grit Goal Wheel

The following is a **Grit Goal Wheel**. I designed the wheel because I wanted to build my life based on what was important to me. The Grit Goal Wheel reflects the life I want to live. Putting attention, energy and effort into things that don't connect to your dreams, your goals and your desires are a waste of your attention. Each morning I write my dreams into my Grit Goal Wheel. It helps me to stay focused on what I want to put my attention on. It keeps my thoughts aligned with my objectives and dreams, and reminds me that I control my destiny.

Wheel Guide:

I want greatness in all of these areas, so this is where I put my attention: **Family, Business/Money, Health, BHAG, and my Grit List.**

FAMILY: I want to enjoy love and greatness when I walk in the door at my home each night. In order to enjoy that, I have to make family my number one priority.

BUSINESS/MONEY: I want greatness in my business and in my net worth. My business is a representation of me and my team. Net worth is the scoreboard of the results. Therefore, I spend a lot of time focusing on this area of my life.

HEALTH: I have not always been concerned about health, but as I get older, I have. The healthier I am, the better my life is. I want to focus on working out, eating right, and moving my body everyday.

Big, Hairy, Audacious, Goals (BHAG): In order for me to stay 100% interested in my life I need *monster* goals to reach for. In their book, *Built to Last,* authors Jim Collins and Jerry Porras coined the perfect term for these goals: Big, Hairy, Audacious Goals (BHAG). BHAG's are what put people on the moon or create the tallest buildings in the world. To most they are outlandish and ridiculous, but to people with Grit, BHAG's are motivation.

GRIT LIST: I get tremendous pleasure from reading, writing, sharing ideas and reflecting. I want to spend time each day on this.

Thats it, just 4 areas that I consider worthy of massive attention and focus. Every morning I write what I want from each, and I spend my day accomplishing them. Try this for just one week. The results you see and feel will be amazing.

Use this Grit Goal Wheel as an example. Write your goals and dreams on each line. Tweak it, make it your own and refer to it daily:

FAMILY

BUSINESS | MONEY

BHAG

GRIT LIST
I AM...

HEALTH

☐ READING

☐ WRITING

☐ SHARING

☐ REFLECTING

DAILY GRIT GOAL WHEEL

5

GRIT TAKES MORE THAN ONE STEP

How many times have you watched a TV infomercial for some simple product solution and said to yourself, "Why didn't I think of that?"

You might have. You may have even taken the first step to launching it. But that's the problem. **You only took the first step, and in the world of Grit, that doesn't count for much.**

Grit (and success in business) is the ability to stay the course and take the second, third, fourth, fifth step and beyond— the steps that actually get things done. Let's apply this TV infomercial principle to your business.

Let's say you wanted to go after a new market that you thought was untapped. So you bought a list of names and leads and built a plan that would start first thing on Monday. You told everyone that Monday couldn't come soon enough for you to conquer the market and become the king or queen of the industry.

When Monday came, you were at your desk. You made 10 calls, then something came up and you got sidetracked, caught up in the day-to-day running of your business rather than following your dream.

Monday turned into a wash out and on Tuesday you just couldn't get the mojo going. You couldn't get it going the day after, either. And you eventually quit.

You made the classic mistake that most people without real Grit make: you took the first step and nothing more. You didn't even give it a real shot, let alone stay in the fight long enough to see real change.

Your Mama Had it Wrong

When your mother told you the most important step was the first step, **she was wrong**. In a Gritty world, the most important steps are the second, third, fourth, fifth step and beyond.

The first steps of the journey to business success don't tell you much, nor do they test your Grit. Meeting with a lawyer to set up your incorporation papers hardly counts as being in business. Getting business cards printed and attending a networking luncheon? Amateur hour. Setting up a twitter account and tweeting twice a week...really?

Understand this: While the first step is important, continuing to take steps in the direction of your goals and dreams, consistently over time (sometimes a long time) is what matter most.

Don't Let Fear of Failure OR Success Stop You

It's scary to go for your goals. But fear of failure is not always the culprit. Sometimes we are actually **afraid of success**.

The boxer Mike Tyson said that when he became heavyweight champion of the world, his posse of friends could no long afford to hang with him. He didn't care, he just wanted his posse around him, and so he would pay for all of them to travel the globe. They were riding his coattails.

But the fact is, paying for his friends didn't fix the situation or address his issues surrounding wealth. His friends resented him and made him feel guilty over his success. And because he couldn't reconcile his relationship with success, he did what a lot of people do in this situation: He lost it. He ultimately sabotaged his own success—went into debt and filed for bankruptcy. In other words, returned to his roots: Hungry, broke, fighting and surrounded by people just like him.

Sound crazy? It's not. The fear of actually succeeding can stop you in your tracks.

The fear of failure and the fear of success are both excuses. The reality is that you didn't have the Grit to see it through, so you bailed out. Stay the course and keep moving forward by taking decisive action, step-by-step.

> ### GRIT TIP
> *The first step doesn't count for much in a world of Grit. It's the second, third, fourth, fifth and beyond that really count.*

My point is this: If you don't take decisive action, day in and day out, over a long period of time, you may (make that will) allow your fear to drive your choices, and that means subconsciously choosing things that are bad for your business and your life, *even if you think you want something different.*

The key is to face those fears and own up to what's holding you back, so that you can be 100% sure that your decisions line up with the outcome you want—not the thing you fear most.

Big goals help you avoid this trap. Once you know where you are going, and have a roadmap based on your goals and dreams, magic happens. Then, you can actually start achieving the business and life you have dreamed of having.

6

BORROW SOME GRIT

Make sure you have done your homework before you start your small business. If you are up and running, **it's time to give your business knowledge a major check-up.**

Here is a new rule in today's marketplace: Experts only.

QUESTION: Why is it that every top athlete has a coach, but most business owners don't?

ANSWER: You don't want to master your craft as much as they do, and that's why you have not reached the pinnacle of your career. You are still, sorry to say, an amatuer. Today, experts get paid, while amateurs get crushed. Developing more skills in business is *not* something you can do without if you want to reach your maximum level of Grittiness.

When the chips are down, it's your skills, your mastery, and the confidence that comes from that mastery that gives you the

confidence to fight another day. It's also how you make the most money.

For example, if you own a towing company, but you don't know the difference between towing a clunker from a Ferrari, you won't make as much money as someone who does; PERIOD. The market will look at you as an amateur and not as an expert and over time, it will feed you to the dogs.

You are required to put in the time and effort to understand every aspect of how your business works, or you risk getting burned. Being in business in today's world means more than just owning a business—it means having a deep skill set that includes **sales, legal, insurance, licensing, accounting, marketing, social media, human resources, information technology**, and more.

You need to learn everything you can about everything that impacts your industry and how to make the industry work for you. And while you need to hire stellar employees so that you don't have to do every job on your own, that does not mean you have the luxury of not knowing how to do every job.

Don't Get Burned

If you think where you are today is good enough, you are going to get burned. A new law will be enacted that radically changes your

industry. A new, larger competitor from China will enter your market with pricing that blows you out of the water. Constantly be on the lookout for new ways to enhance your skills, your product offerings, and your levels of service so that you are not caught off guard.

Here is a dirty little secret of your employees: Some of them think you're an idiot. Some of them think that you couldn't live without them, and eventually, some of them will try to test their theory.

We've all heard horror stories of how a business owner went bankrupt because a bookkeeper embezzled from him, or of a business owner who's top dog salesperson up and left and took all of his clients with him. When this happens, *it's your fault*. You went easy on your Grit and you got burned.

Those stories are sad but true—they happen all the time in business. But your job is to have so much Grit, so much in the pipeline, so much abundance, that if it happens to you, you can survive.

I'm a sales guy, through and through. I'm not a CPA. But trust me: once a week in my office, my bookkeeper prints me an updated copy of our balance sheet and income statement and I go through it with a fine-toothed comb. I have no formal training in

accounting , but I know enough about accounting and financial statements to read mine every week. You need to be able to do the same.

If you are a master mechanic with unmatched skills, but you can't read a bank statement, you are going to get burned. It's not enough to be great at your specific job. If you are a small business owner in today's fast paced environment, you need to have a thorough understanding of all aspects of the business in order to survive.

Read As Much as You Can

The average CEO reads 4 to 5 books per month, and earns 536 times more than the average book reader makes in a year. The average book reader buys 1 book per year and 60% of them don't read past the first chapter. Who do you think is expanding their skills for business?

What are you reading or listening to? Who do you look up to? I have been interested in interesting people my entire life. Biographies of successful people give me skills, insight, and motivation, and I need that often.

Most people don't need this constant flow of motivation, and I often get criticized for my thirst for more knowledge. But I know

when I hear that from people, it only means one thing: They don't have *The Grit*. The biggest, best minds in business are constantly reading, attending seminars, and listening for inspiration. If you are not one of them, you are failing yourself, your business, and your family.

My friends used to give me a hard time because I drove a 2003 Lexus LS 430 for too long. They told me I needed a new car:

"You can't take a client out in that!"

"You can't pull up to valet in that!"

"Would you take your wife to dinner in that?"

"Is that the best you can do, Manero?"

I told them to screw off. The truth is I had hundreds of audio tapes that I had collected and listened to for the past 25 years, and they didn't make new cars with tape decks. I wanted the information inside those tapes more than I wanted the impression a nicer car would give me.

During the great recession of 2008 and 2009, my tapes and (paid-for) Lexus, got me through. The stories I heard on those

tapes gave me strategies, and they gave me hope. In my darkest hours, where my Grit has been tested the most, it's has been my skill, my mentors on tape, and my unyielding confidence that got me through.

Can you name the last 6 books you read or listened to? How about just the *last* book? *Is* there a last book? Reading

> ## GRIT TIP
> *Connect with other Gritty people. You are who you surround yourself with.*

and learning are undeniable habits of successful, Gritty people.

The Grittiest people I know are searching for something: significance, attention, or maybe avoidance of pain—pain caused by a loss in most cases. But the point is they are fighting like hell to achieve something to fill the void. Most people look at losses like a problem or a weakness. But for me, they have always been opportunities.

I have turned losses into an opportunities, because I have constantly been looking for people I can look up to: people I can learn from; people who can inspire me. Whether I know these people or not, I can learn from them. While I may not have had hundreds of personal mentors, I have had hundreds of meaningful mentors from the thousands of books and tapes I have read and listened to over the years.

Make a commitment to yourself to learn from others, and you will see your skills, your confidence, and your business improve.

Recommended reading list:

- ❏ *The 10x Rule* by Grant Cardone
- ❏ *The E Myth* by Michael Gerber
- ❏ *Swim With the Sharks Without Being Eaten Alive* by Harvey Mackay
- ❏ *Street Smarts* by Norm Brodsky
- ❏ *Person of Interest* by Micheal Burt
- ❏ *Mr. Shmooze* by Richard Abraham
- ❏ *How to Win at the Sport of Business* by Mark Cuban
- ❏ *Purple Cow* by Seth Godin
- ❏ *Built to Last* by Jim Collins and Jerry Porras
- ❏ *Good to Great* by Jim Collins
- ❏ *Mastering The Rockefeller Habits* by Verne Harnish
- ❏ *7 Habits of Highly Effective People* by Stephen Covey

7

FIND YOUR GRIT NICHE

The business marketplace today is cloudy and crowded. For example: got an idea to start a hamburger joint that serves cheap food fast? Try again. Want to serve gourmet coffee in a white cup with a logo and charge $3 a serving? Good luck.

Because so many business ideas and concepts are in place already, you need to work hard to find your niche. **Businesses who try to do everything for everyone don't make it anymore.** Remember, experts only please. You need to have a niche in your business that separates you from the competition. Once you have separated yourself from the competition, **you need to market yourself as the expert in this niche, so you can be noticed.**

Finding My Niche

When I started my first business, I knew that there was money in the equipment finance industry. I realized very early on that large

banks and finance companies loved financing new commercial fleet vehicles.

I didn't understand the "niche" concept fully yet, so I created my first company, Commercial Fleet Financing, Inc. (CFF) to focus on, guess what? Financing *new* commercial fleet vehicles. I was up against huge, publically traded companies, and I didn't have a snowball's chance in hell.

After a few years of failing to gain traction and growth, I realized I needed to rethink my strategy in order to survive. I looked at my happiest clients, and my most profitable deals, and realized that they all had one thing in common: ***used equipment***.

It became clear to me that my competition—large, publicly traded banks—didn't want to finance used equipment. **In that moment, my niche was born.**

> ### GRIT TIP
> *Just because you're small doesn't mean you won't be successful. Embrace your underdog status, find your niche, and be the leading expert.*

I decided CFF would be the best used equipment financing company on the planet. Although we still finance new equipment,

CFF is now known as a leader in used equipment financing. **Understanding our niche, and marketing ourselves as the expert in this niche, saved my business.** You need to find the same type of niche for your business.

The key to winning business in a niche market is twofold:

#1. Become an expert in your niche.

To become an expert, skill up and cover all of your bases in your chosen niche. This may require additional licenses, bonds, certifications, ratings and background checks. Customers will pay for expertise, but you have to do the work first, because but they can see a phony coming a mile away. It's worth it to do the work, because as an expert, you can charge more and **will be paid more.** Remember: Amateurs get crushed; experts get paid.

#2. Market yourself as the expert.

It's not enough to be just be an expert in your niche. You need to own it, and market yourself as an expert. Everything you do, from your business cards, email signature lines, media materials, brochures, websites, social media, and even the sign on your door, must tell the marketplace that you are an expert. The best customers are not looking for what you are selling—they are

looking for your expertise. If Tiger Woods was looking for a golf coach, he could find one on any course in the country. But he wanted the best, so he found Butch Harmon.

To find your niche, ask yourself these questions:

- Why do my best customers do business with me?
- What are my competitors *not* doing that I *can* do?
- Can I run my business *better* than the current players?
- Is this niche a flash-in-the-pan or a long-term business?

Pick a niche, market yourself as the expert in this niche and continue to look for new opportunities within the niche. Remember, amateurs don't get paid—experts in niche markets do.

8

BUILD A GRITTY COMPANY CULTURE

For the first ten years of my twenty years as a business owner, I had clients, revenue, expenses, and employees— *but I still didn't have a company*. Why? Because a business means you have a group of people doing various jobs; a company has culture, a mission, something to identify with. We didn't grow as quickly as we could have, had we been a company first.

Despite our limited financial success, we had foundational problems caused by lack of focus and employee turnover.

So I decided over a decade ago that I wanted to recreate CFF as a company that put company culture first.

> ### GRIT TIP
>
> *A company of one person still needs a clear company culture. No company culture—no company.*

From that moment on, we have hired like-minded people who want greatness in all areas of their life, created an incredible customer experience, and developed a compensation program that provides abundance for our employees. The decision to build a great company with clearly

defined company culture has been wildly successful for my company over the past decade. Without question, it has made a huge impact on my success and will on yours, too, if you do it the right way.

The Power of Company Culture

There are limited guarantees in business, but here is one I will bet the ranch on: **no company culture, no company.**

Company culture affects every aspect of a business. It's the heartbeat of the organization. Your employees, customers, and community are craving it. You may have a business that has revenue, expenses and employees, but without a clearly defined company culture, you don't have a company—you just have a business.

Here are 4 important ways to create a winning company culture within your organization:

1. Fire the PR Firm

Company culture comes from the top down. You, your partners, and your managers set the tone. Your staff, just like your customers, can sense phoniness, so fire the PR firm and figure this one out on your own. Take some time, sit down with a pen and

paper, and get serious about how you want to design or redesign your company. Don't get crazy here with long drawn out mission statements or core value plaques that hang from every corner. Keep your values simple and easy, but make sure your team understands them and agrees to them BEFORE you hire them.

Ask yourself these questions:

- ❑ Who are we? What do we stand for?
- ❑ What type of personalities work for us?
- ❑ Why would someone want to work for us VS. our competitors?
- ❑ What do the best employees in our industry want? How can we provide this for them and recruit them to work for us?
- ❑ What do we want our employees to tell their families and friends about our organization?
- ❑ What do we want the employee and customer experience with us to feel like?
- ❑ How does our company contribute to the local economy and community?

Below are the core values that I operate my businesses with. I created these when I decided to get serious about company culture back in 2001. **These core values are simple, powerful ideas that have stood the test of time for my businesses:**

 CORE VALUES Est.2001

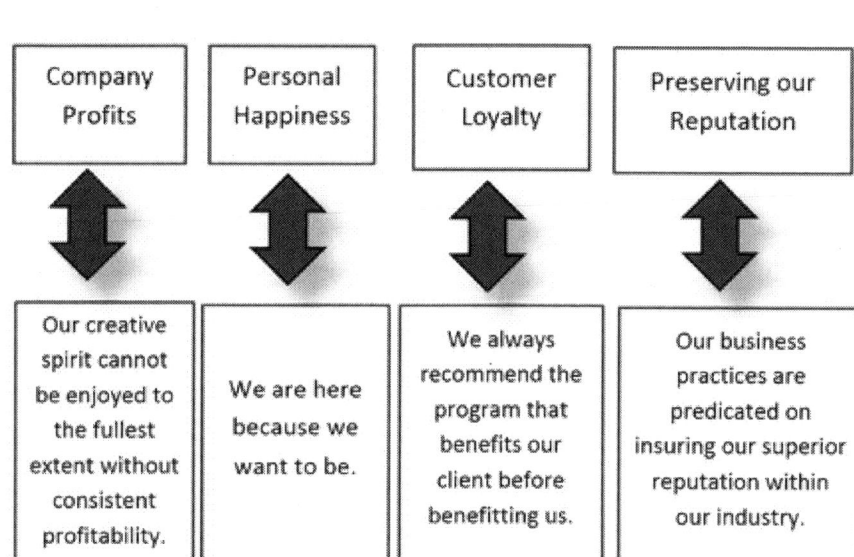

Company Profits	Personal Happiness	Customer Loyalty	Preserving our Reputation
Our creative spirit cannot be enjoyed to the fullest extent without consistent profitability.	We are here because we want to be.	We always recommend the program that benefits our client before benefitting us.	Our business practices are predicated on insuring our superior reputation within our industry.

2. Get Out of Your Office

Regardless of the type of business you are in, your employees need to see you walking around and paying attention. Harvey Mackay, author of *Swim With the Sharks Without Being Eaten Alive*, said it best: "You have to walk the factory floor daily."

Use your daily walk around the office or factory as a time in which you point out success rather than failures. **Key point:** When you do this daily walk around, you *must* keep this time positive, so your employees will feel good about their work.

Never, I repeat, *never* use this time to point out problems or weaknesses to them. You want them to feel good about their work and the company they have chosen to work for. Do this exercise right and it can create magic. Do it wrong (by pointing out problems) and it will destroy the culture you are trying to build.

3. Schedule a Daily "Scrum" For Your Team

Every working day at CFF, we have a companywide meeting that we call our "scrum." It starts at 9:30 a.m. and lasts for no more than 10 minutes. During that time, the phones go to voicemail, the outbound calls stop, and we all gather around the conference table.

We always discuss our results from the previous day and determine what we should expect from each other for today. Sometimes we play a quick training video. The most important thing is that we take a few minutes to focus on the day ahead together.

I know that in most companies, it seems impossible to do a companywide meeting. But is it really impossible?

If I told you that sales could double in the next twelve months because of a ten-minute per day meeting, would you find a way to make it happen?

Chances are yes. **And that's exactly what happened at my office in 2013 and 2014.** Our annual fundings went from $36,000,000 to $100,000,000, due largely in part to the company-wide attitude refresh brought about by our new mandatory daily scrum.

If you are convinced that you can't do a companywide meeting, then plan a daily department meeting. You, as the boss, could even attend each department meeting to help spread your company culture. Remember, **culture comes from the top down**.

4. Create Competition

Your team needs new motivation to close more deals. Sorry to tell you this, but your business gets **boring**. It's not as exciting to others as it is to you, and you need to constantly create an environment that keeps it interesting and fun.

Create a competition each day, week, month, or quarter that focuses on something meaningful to the company or department.

The prize does not need to be big money, it could simply be a pizza party or a gift card to Starbucks. In my companies, among other awards, we give simple ribbons that say **#1, Winner, or Best**. We now have them hanging all around our office.

Your team needs something to motivate them to sell more, produce more, or deliver more—so make sure to create it for them. It's about keeping the energy level high, not about breaking the bank.

Here are some examples of competitions you can start today:

➢ Who can smile the biggest
➢ Best new idea of the day
➢ Worlds greatest attitude for the day
➢ Most on-site client visits for the week
➢ Most cold calls in one day
➢ Most calls to existing clients in one day
➢ Most video thank-you's sent to existing clients
➢ Highest revenue producer for the quarter
➢ Highest profit producer for the month
➢ Most repeat customer orders
➢ Most units shipped for the week

You get the picture. A competition keeps the work environment interesting and exciting. If you can keep your company full of that atmosphere, you are on your way to bigger revenue and success.

9

MOTIVATE YOUR EMPLOYEES TO BE GRITTY

If you are a Gritty employer, you will want to make members of your staff Gritty too. Once you have built a company culture that represents your vision, it's time to get your people on board.

You must lead by example. There is not one job in any of my companies that I have not done. I will get in the trenches at any time if anyone needs help. Everyone in my office knows that I care about their success, and that I want them to achieve greatness.

I'll let you in on another secret: your employees secretly love to be pushed. It's your job as the Gritty employer to get the best out of them. You will get the benefit too, but you need to want it for them first. They want to do better, and they want more for themselves and their families. You, as the Gritty leader, need to help them get there.

It's your job to create an opportunity for them that they can't get elsewhere. The great ones get it quickly and require less of

your time and skill, but batting 1000% is impossible. Some employees don't speak up. They will just do what everyone else is doing, even though they are capable of doing more.

In some cases, the worst employees have the biggest mouths and can bully the weaker employees.

Many small business owners are pushovers, so they never get the best out of their employees. In many cases, the employees steamroll the employer—they come in late, leave early, do things their way rather than the company way, and miss their monthly sales goals with minimal if any consequences. Don't feel bad if you're a wimpy employer. I used to be one too.

Toughening Up In My Management

My business was about five years old when I realized I needed to fire a telemarketing employee named Larry. I agonized over it. I lost sleep over the fact that I was letting him go—I was afraid of how it might affect his family.

Larry would take his lunch break and multiple smoke breaks in the

back of his van parked in the baking Texas sun in the parking lot. He would come and go as he pleased. He would call in sick without any consequences. He would need to leave early and I always said OK.

He was constantly underperforming. But the truth is I had set no real goals for Larry: no sales quotas, no concrete plan. I had hoped that Larry would work hard enough and make enough calls to find me sorely needed business, but it wasn't happening.

I let things slide until one day I heard Larry talking with total disrespect to a prospect over the phone. Although I didn't know how to manage people at that time, I knew that I wasn't going to let Larry wreck what little reputation I had built up.

When I finally called Larry to the conference room to fire him, he arrived at the table with his briefcase already in hand.

I was shaking I was so nervous, worried if I was making the right decision. *I don't have a replacement for him. I really need someone to find me more business, maybe I should give him a second chance,* I was saying in my head. But then I remembered

the way he was talking to the prospective client.

"Larry, I'm going to let you go," I said.

Larry got up from the table, grabbed his briefcase and with a smirk on his face, said, "You should have fired me three weeks ago!"

Can you imagine that? I was paying him before I was paying myself to make sure he was happy, while the whole time he was giving me the minimum effort and taking from me and my meager bank account.

Set Your Standards High

That was the end of wimpy Matt the manager. **From that moment on, I have required everyone that works for me to reach a high standard—that I set for them.** I have done every job in my business many times over. I know my business inside and out, and I know the levels of performance required.

Every employee in my companies is given a very detailed job description that outlines the duties of their job. I'm happy to make adjustments if needed, but I set the bar at the level I want rather than at the level they want. This point is key: **You must lead your people or they will take the path of least resistance.**

Some know exactly what they are doing, milking the system and your checkbook week in and week out. And some don't. They just don't know how to push themselves for better performance and greater contribution. That's why you must lead people in the direction you want, *or they will lead you in the direction they want*.

Some people won't make it. The level I set is higher than their current skill set and they don't do enough to get better. In many cases, even though they want to be pushed to new levels, it scares them. I have zero tolerance for doing less work because of that mindset. You and I are writing the checks, rolling the dice, and taking the risk. We have every right to set

GRIT TIP

You want to work around people who want what you want. Find like-minded people, hire them, and then lead them.

the bar high, and they have an obligation to reach that bar.

Details Are Everything

Without a clear job description, you are being unfair—you can't have expectations of someone without explaining those expectations to them first. **You must outline the functions of the job in explicit detail, and then push your people to reach it.** I pay over $20,000 a year for what I think is the world's greatest online motivational and sales training program and make it available to everyone all year, both at home and at work 24/7.

I have a mentoring program where our new employees work underneath our veterans to learn the business. In my office, you can't get half-pregnant. When you are on our team, you get access to everything I can throw at you to make you a better trained, more highly skilled, and more Gritty employee.

In the end, you can lead a horse to water but you can't make it drink. If your employees don't want what to take advantage of the opportunity, training and culture you are offering, you need to say goodbye.

Here is the key in that situation—don't be a jerk. Call them in and let them know that it's not working out, but that you have a real desire to help them be successful. In the end, if they don't turn the performance around, it's time to part ways. Part of my management style is to try to go through my contacts and make calls to people I know who might be looking for someone with their skill set. If I can help them move on with dignity, I want to do so.

Grit doesn't mean being a jerk. **Grit means having the guts to make the tough calls, including firing underperforming employees.**

10
NO EXCUSES. PERIOD.

I operate with a **"no excuses" mentality.** This is not just for me, but also for my staff. You need to do the same thing. You are playing a risky game here and it's called your business. In order for you to get Gritty, you must adopt a "No Excuses" policy.

Close the circle

Take a look in your garage. Do you have lots of projects that were started but not finished? These projects are actually "circles" that have not been closed. Why? Because we make excuses. "I ran out of time" or I will get to it later" are excuses...they are NOT VALID and in a gritty world, they cost you opportunities, happiness and money. Now look at your office. Do you have marketing efforts that were started but not finished. Do you have prospecting calls that need to be made? How about employment ads for new people that have not been placed yet? Excuses are distractions, and distractions get in the way of completion. Embrace this quote "If I can't then I must." Remove ALL excuses from your mindset. If you commit to anything, *do* anything to

close the circle and complete it. Pick up the phone **NOW** and make the call you need to make. Don't let excuses like "It's too early", or "It's lunch time" or "It's too late" to stop you from closing the circle. The most productive calls are made early, at lunchtime or late in the day. Make it easy on yourself and think of it like this...once you start something, you have started a new circle, and that circle must get closed. Unclosed circles keep you up at night, disorganized and unfocused. They also provide an opportunity for Gritty competitors to steal business from you.

Get to Work, No Matter What

A few years ago, we embarked on a massive IT project in my office. When we were a smaller company, I hired a team of programmers to build me a backend system we call "Golden Gate." It was a program that systematized our business and made it easier to manage all aspects—part CRM, part sales machine, part accounting assistant. It was perfect, but over time, we simply outgrew it.

With our growth, this necessary system had become outdated. I wanted to enhance and redo Golden Gate. The original group of programmers has disbanded, so I needed to build a new team. A former IT manager had tried to redo the system, but failed.

THE GRIT

BY MATT MANERO

The new version of Golden Gate was dormant for 2 years before our new IT manager stepped up. **This time we scoped the project in detail with very clear job descriptions and timelines for the team**. We were making great progress and needed to keep pushing on our timeline.

On an important system test day, my IT manager operating as our project leader, called to tell me that his dog was eaten by a coyote during the night, and he wasn't coming in.

What would you have said? Would you have said, "I understand. Take the day off to handle things"?

Not if you run with a no-excuses mindset. I told him to get his ass to work. I know it sounds harsh. But I don't accept excuses from myself, or anyone else, especially when the stakes are high. I work when I'm sick, tired, fed-up and pissed-off and I expect the same from my team.

> ### GRIT TIP
> *Excuses short change your dreams. Remove excuses from the equation.*

If you and I are on the same team, I will run through fire for you and I expect you to do the same for me. You can't operate with a no-excuses attitude some of the time. You must operate with a no-excuses attitude all of the time. And this means that you must make tough calls like this.

My IT manager came to the office that day, and I expressed both my sorrow for his dog and my thanks for him showing tremendous Grit.

We completed the project that day successfully, and the company culture was established even more firmly—with a higher bar set for the other employees.

A no excuses policy only works if you **lead by a no excuses example.** Don't be the leader that talks the talk and doesn't walk the walk - it kills company culture. Don't leave the office at noon on Friday just because you can. If your employees are required to come in on Saturday...guess what? You need to work a bunch of Saturday's. And for goodness sake, if your company dress code is business casual, don't buck the rule and walk around in flip flops and shorts. Your team hates that type of non Gritty leadership.

If you want a dedicated, Gritty company culture, you have to walk a Gritty walk. Even when it's hard, especially when it's hard.

11
GENERATE REVENUE, REVENUE, REVENUE

You have been given the wrong advice most of your life. People say, "Watch the pennies and the dollars will come." Hogwash. **You need to generate BIG revenue first.**

Most business owners spend too much time focusing on their expenses and too little time looking at how they can grow revenue. Watching expenses is important, but if you do not have increasing revenue, the expenses will not matter.

Revenue Rule #1: Revenue growth is essential to any business.

The idea that most businesses fail because they do not have enough startup capital or enough contacts is wrong. Most businesses fail because they do not generate enough

> ### GRIT TIP
> *More revenue equals more sales. Everyone in your organization is a salesperson, regardless of their job title. Make the need for more sales and revenue **a top priority**.*

revenue to keep the doors open. Revenue comes from sales and relationships. You and your team need to learn how to sell your products, hold your pricing, and **find more business.**

Revenue rule #2: Shit happens. Be prepared for it.

Your customers may go out of business. Your contacts may get fired, or your customers may lose a key account that is out of your control. Whatever the setback, a growing stream of revenue helps you to be prepared for any bump in the road.

Don't wait until the shit hits the fan to react. In most cases, by that point it will be too late. **Stay focused on revenue generation all the time—not just some of the time.**

Revenue rule #3: Generating revenue is about effort and action.

Here is one thing I know for sure: you are not taking enough action. You might think you are pushing, but I know that you have another gear, and deep down you know it too. Once you have determined your niche, go into **Massive Action Mode.**

How? Take out your calendar and fill it up. Pack in as much activity as you can. If you make 10 calls a day, you now need to be

www.mattmanero.com

74

making 100 calls a day—10X your day, as bestselling author Grant Cardone says. If you have 20 clients, you need 200—stop seeking upward limits and instead seek ways to push through them. Don't believe this lie in your head that what you want isn't attainable. *More really is more.* More clients, more revenue and more profits matter.

Make a list of potential customers, call them today (and everyday), and ask for their business. It could actually be that easy. ***"Mr. Jones, this is Matt Manero with Commercial Fleet in Dallas. I have identified you as a perfect client for my company and I want to earn your business..."*** is the call I make often. And it works more times than it fails. This simple one sentence gets me appointments that lead to more revenue. Go ahead, try it in your business and watch your sales increase. Go see your existing customers in person, build a deep relationship with them, and remind them that you are an expert. Because of your expertise, you can show them how to run a better business. Do not think that they will assume this. You need to remind them, and remind them often.

Revenue Rule #4: Keep a constant pipeline of new contacts.

Your pipeline of customers and new business opportunities is the lifeline of your business. Visiting and constantly staying in front of your customers is the easiest way to build and sustain a healthy pipeline. The best place to find more business is by talking to your existing clients. Call each client every 30 days *at a minimum*. Never take your current clients for granted. Show them *massive* amounts of love, and push for more revenue from them at every opportunity.

Create an email campaign to your client base, write a blog, max out your effort on social media, text and call your clients, create short videos on Youtube, send them interesting articles and do a direct mail campaign every quarter. These actions do not take a lot of time or money, and you can't always quantify the results. But trust, me, they are **high value activities**. You need to stay in front of your customers, or someone else will.

Revenue Rule #5: Think about MORE.

Never stop thinking about how you can do more. **More customer contacts, more networking, more relationships.** More effort means more revenue. Over deliver on everything you do. Never do the bare minimum. Value can be added so easily today

because so few companies offer it. Thank you cards, educational articles, and personal visits are just a few quick and easy ways to add value without breaking the bank.

Sometimes Gritty actions don't require you to push a rock up hill. Some can actually be easy and painless. Here is a perfect example. Ask yourself this, "When was the last time you bought something and after the purchase, you received a thank you card from the salesperson?" My guess is rarely, very rarely. Thank you cards create a simple, yet magical opportunity for us all. They also separate us from the competition. Why? Because our competitors don't do it, therefore we must do it. Go to the stationary store today and buy some cards that say THANK YOU on them. Handwrite a note, put a stamp on it and mail it. The results will be magical and the cost is less than $1.00 each. Ask yourself, "Where else can I do these ridiculously inexpensive actions that create tremendous value with my customers and separate me from my competition?" Search these activities out, act on them, and do them for a long period of time.

12

FORCE A GRITTY PROFIT MARGIN

Sooner or later, if you are going to make it in your business, you are going to have to dip into your reserves to take advantage of an opportunity. The key question is: **Do you have reserves to dip into?**

Forcing your business to produce a higher profit margin will help you build up *and fund* a reserve account. **Business, after all, never goes straight up.**

If you start small, you have limited expenses and you can survive on minimal revenue and profits. However, as the business grows, the profitability of your business will become a real factor.

When you reach a certain size you need to make sure that your business operates at a reasonable profit margin **AFTER YOU HAVE PAID YOURSELF.** Your business must make a profit after all bills have been paid, including your own salary.

Don't Just Trade Dollars

The scary part about many businesses is that they are just trading dollars. If you can't operate your business with a free and clear profit margin **AFTER YOU PAY YOURSELF**, you are just trading dollars.

If your business just trades dollars, you don't have real profits. All you have is money coming in the front door, checks being written that empty the bank accounts and get mailed out the back door. This type of business will fail over time.

Different businesses have different margins, but **I suggest, at a bare minimum, a 10% profit margin as a starting base line.** If you want to increase your profit margin because you can, then go for it. But we need to start somewhere, and 10% is a good starting point. But as you will see below, generating the profit margin is not good enough. Gritty business owners understand that putting their profits into a reserve account is how the players win in business.

GRIT TIP

A reserve account is critical to your long-term viability. Force your business to operate at a respectable profit margin, then hoard the cash in your reserve account.

You have to build a reserve, and reserves are not credit lines. Reserves are real cash in the bank: sacred cash, hoarded cash, that just sits and waits to be used. Bank credit lines are credit, and credit can be tough find when you need it most. Your banker might be happy to give you a credit line when your financials and cash flow look strong, but when it gets tight, there's no assurance your credit line will be renewed. You need real cash in the bank.

Each and every dollar your business produces as revenue must generate a minimum of a 10% profit margin. I want your business to generate even more than 10%, but you have to start somewhere. If you want to increase your required profit margin to 20%, 25%, or more, then you should.

By the Numbers

In our 10% example: if you bring in $100,000 per year in revenue, your business has $10,000 of profit left over as **REAL PROFIT—after you pay yourself.** It's called **PROFIT.**

If your business brings in $1,000,000 per year in revenue, you have $100,000 left over and if you bring in $10,000,000 per year, you have $1,000,000 left over.

Now is where it gets harder: **You need to have 2 bank accounts**. The first account is your operating account in which the revenue comes in, the expenses go out and your 10% profit is left over, waiting for you to do something with it. Now the tough part: you must transfer the 10% out of your operating account and into your new second account, called your "reserve" account.

I call this account "reserve" because you will likely need to tap into it in the future: A competitor goes out of business and you can buy their inventory on the cheap—you need the reserves to be able to do this. A new warehouse or office space opens up for you to buy or expand—you need reserves to make this happen too. Or maybe, your business hits a bump in the road and your profits get slashed—you need a reserve account built up to cover the red ink.

Transfer the 10% profit margin from your operating account into your reserve account each week. It's simple to do with the click of a button. Remember, it is not enough to just cover your bills. You need REAL PROFITS that are transferred into a separate RESERVE account. Your balance sheet should now list two accounts: one is your "operating account" and the other is now your "reserve" account. Your operating account covers your bills (including your salary) and your reserve account keeps the profit

margin, safe, secure, and waiting. **This point is key;** by transferring your profit margin out of your operating account, you remove the luxury that extra cash provides. When you have too much cash in your operating account, you can be lulled to sleep, into a false sense of security. Once you remove the profit from your operating account your ending balance will look smaller, and that is what you want. Remember, **we are looking for ways to stay Gritty in our business, and small bank balances are one way to make that happen.** Your reserve account is just that, a reserve, a rainy day fund. It's not a "vacation fund" or a "don't tell my wife" fund. It's hard earned profits that have been put aside and earmarked for "future use".

I have used this process for years now, and it's saved my business and allowed me to make strategic growth moves when they present themselves. Don't be lazy when it comes to forcing your business to run a maximum profit margin. **Get out of the trading dollars business and into the profit-generating business.**

13

CREATE A GRITTY TEAM OF ADVISORS

When I started my business in 1995, I was told not to trust anyone. I was told, "Only one hand works the register," and "Only you handle the books."

Due to this thinking, I didn't trust anyone. I never hired a great accountant, lawyer, insurance agent, or business advisor. I was missing out on having strong advisors, and my business was suffering for it. I thought I could, and should, do it all on my own.

WRONG. I needed a strong team of advisors to support my business, and so do you. These people are on your team to make you better. *They work for you* and they must have your best interest in mind.

Here are the players to select for your team: **an accountant, a lawyer, an insurance agent, a finance partner, and an advisor.**

1. **Accountant**

   It is your duty to pay your taxes, but not a penny more than you should. You need a good accountant, either on staff or at an outside company, to help manage your income, expenses, profits, and taxes. Find a good accountant, update them every month, and keep accurate books. Equally important is that your accountant makes recommendations for you. He or she must be a Gritty, out-of-the-box thinker if they are going to help you maximize your profits. I want everything you do to be 100% above board, but a Gritty accountant knows about strategies, ideas, and concepts that can help you in driving your business into the proper lower tax and higher profit zone.

2. **Insurance Agent**

   Your insurance agent must be an expert in your industry because they should be making recommendations to protect you. Ask about types of general liability, product liability, life insurance, health insurance, downtime coverage, breakdown coverage, gap insurance, and even

disability insurance. Make sure you have enough coverage so that your assets are protected in case of disaster.

3. **Lawyer**

You don't need a nice lawyer—you need a tough, nasty, Gritty lawyer. Your lawyer is going to do the dirty work for you when called upon, and you don't want a wimp. You need someone willing to be tough and demanding. Be proactive in finding the right lawyer. Have a good lawyer lined up, build a relationship with them, so that if and when an issue arises, you can call them and they will already know you and your business.

4. **Finance partner**

Build a relationship with your banker or finance partner before you need them. If you land a new contract, you want to be able to move quickly. You want your finance partner, if needed, to issue credit quickly. You need to prepare for this in advance. A finance partner can be your banker, or an independent finance company. Either way, you need them to understand your business and offer quality recommendations and be able to pull the *approved* trigger when you need it most.

5. **Advisor**

Would you go to a marriage counselor who has been married and divorced 3 times? Think about it. You need to find someone in your industry who has accomplished *what you want to accomplish*. Get to know them and develop a relationship with them. These type of people can be key in offering guidance and industry-specific support. Additionally, your advisor should have contacts in the industry. **This is critical,** they can also help you with introductions to other successful people.

You should speak with all the members of your team once a quarter. Whether you need them or not, make the call to them every few months and give your them a status update to keep your business running smoothly. Keeping a few trusted advisors will put you in a good place if, and when, you need help, recommendations and gritty advice.

> ### GRIT TIP
> *If you hang around broke people, you will be broke. If you hang around middle class people, you will be middle class. If you hang around rich people, you will be rich.*

14

BE A BEAR AND FEED UPSTREAM

When it comes to nature, bears are the toughest competitors out there. You need to emulate their model in your own business. Bears are the strongest natural example of pursuing your business with Grit. Here's why (and it all starts with salmon):

Salmon swim upstream and return to the parts of the river where they were born. Many animals hunt the salmon as they swim, including bears.

> **GRIT TIP**
> *Leave the calm waters of scarcity and move upstream toward abundance.*

The strongest and toughest bears go to the part of the stream that causes the most trouble for the salmon to cross: the waterfall.

The stream runs hard here. The rocks are slippery and dangerous. The hardiest bears know that because of the danger, this part of the stream is the least crowded. Here the salmon jump high to

clear the waterfall. The bears sit poised and wait for the salmon to jump, then reach out and catch them in midair.

Unlike the other bears downstream, these Gritty bears take a large, juicy bite out of the salmon and throw the dead salmon back into the stream. **These bears know that because they have risked the most, they reap the biggest reward**: salmon after salmon, mouthful after mouthful. Abundance.

The next group of bears are also smart. Although they are not as Gritty as the first group, they know that the other side of the salmon is still available for them, so they sit and wait a little further downstream. When the half-eaten salmon comes their way, they grab it and eat the other side.

The competition is a little fiercer at this mid-level location, but the salmon are still plentiful. These bears too throw the salmon away and it floats downstream further.

At the bottom of the stream where the rapids end and the water moves slowly, the rest of the animals wait. Here, the foxes, coyotes, birds and rats fight for salmon skeletons. This group fight

over the crumbs. The work is hard because the bones have little meat left and the competition is stiff. Sound familiar?

Are your customers the skeletons of the market? Are your business dealings so low-level that your competition doesn't want them and that's why you are stuck with them? Force yourself to move upstream to find better customers, better employees and more abundance. Find customers who have bigger businesses, more needs, and the ability to provide you with more revenue.

I have told this story so many times in my company that a member of my sales team presented me with a miniature grizzly bear for my desk. I keep it in front of me at all times, as a reminder that **I want to be the Grittiest bear at the most dangerous part of the stream.**

The most dangerous part of the stream, and the toughest part of business—where the competition is the smallest, but the rewards are the greatest. **Abundance awaits the Grittiest.**

Whether a bear in nature or you in your business, abundance awaits the Grittiest of us all. The crumbs await the weakest.

Which bear are you in your business? Fight the temptation for the easy way out. The more you embrace Gritty behavior, by moving upstream, the closer you get to achieving abundance and greatness.

15
STAY PISSED OFF

Think about a time in your life when you were most competitive. It could have been during sports, a test, or even a contest with a sibling. You want to reconnect with this competitive spirit and stay in that competitive state for as long as you can. For me that's what I call my **"constant state of pissed-offness."**

This state causes me to be on my toes. It's like an antenna on the top of my head. I'm always looking, searching, and pushing the envelope. This state also keeps me gritty. **I'm not looking for reasons celebrate—I'm looking for reasons to push even harder.**

You can't go halfway on your journey to having Grit. You can't be Gritty sometimes. If you really want to connect with your Grit, you need to be Gritty all the time. Having Grit means having the ability to *postpone* celebrations.

I often think many people are looking for reasons to celebrate at every turn. Not me, I'm looking for ways to stay Gritty. If we have a successful month in my office, I'm happy to announce that we have something to celebrate. But I keep the celebrating small:

lunch for everyone will be ordered in and served at the conference table, then back to work.

My staff knows that **we are not celebrating the result, we are celebrating the Grit required to create the result.** Our quick celebrations are proof that the fundamentals of Grit actually produced the result we wanted.

Popping champagne and celebrating too much gives you, and your employees, a false sense of the work being "done." It's never done.

Stay Smart in Spending

If your own Grit is eluding you, it could be because you spend too much time looking to reward yourself rather than spending that time developing a strong competitive drive. The last thing you want to be doing is looking for ways to celebrate. Develop a gritty discipline within yourself to work and spend like you are broke- even when you are not.

> ### GRIT TIP
> *Don't celebrate the result. Celebrate that you had the Grit to get you the result.*

I just completed a major renovation to my house: game room, outdoor kitchen, and a sport court for my three young boys. I

reminded my kids, "Your mother and I lived in this house for eight years before we did this. You know why it took us 8 years to give you these luxuries? Because we waited to celebrate. **We postponed our celebration so that we could build this for you without debt."**

I saw house after house get built, completed, and sold in my town. And the people who bought them took on major mortgages to make it happen. But not us.

My motto is: "Let the Jones keep up with the Jones." The Maneros were going to build when we were ready to build. Now I have the nicest house in my neighborhood, with a fraction of the mortgage. Celebrating smart (and rarely) can save you big time in the long run.

Have the Grit to postpone your celebrations and rewards in your business and your personal life, until the time when it's smart for you to indulge. Do everything in your power to never be viewed as the ultimate insult in the great State of Texas, **"He is all hat and no cattle."**

16

MAKE THE GRIT PERSONAL

Grit is not just about your business—it's about the way you live your life. Your Grit will be tested. Often. You need to hold on with Grit when things seem grim. Because here's a secret: You *will* get bored with your business. Your employees *will* let you down and you *will* lose a big, important deal.

You need to already know that these obstacles are coming, and decide to stay in the fight for your business to succeed. It takes Grit to accomplish anything worthwhile in life, but that Grit won't even kick in until you are fighting hard. As you know by now: if it's easy, then it doesn't require Grit.

The lifestyle of Grit is a thought and action process that gives you the confidence to know that no matter what the obstacle in front of you, you can overcome it— but first you have to connect to it. Grit connects to everything worth a damn. Find your Grit. Grab it by the horns and use it to your benefit in everything you do.

THE GRIT

BY MATT MANERO

How Bob Got His Grit Back

For my client Bob, Grit wasn't just a good idea; it saved his life.

I had done millions of dollars of equipment financing deals with Bob over the years, and never realized just how Gritty he was. Grit comes from within, and is often masked by quietness and humility. Very rarely does the big mouth in the crowd have true Grit. They just have a big mouth.

Bob was very overweight and a smoker. So was his wife. Every day, after work, they would come home, sit on the couch with frozen dinners, smoke cigarettes, and watch TV. One night, Bob turned to his wife and said, "We're going to die doing this."

He changed his mind that day about the way he wanted to live his life. He put out his smoke, got up from the couch, and walked down the driveway to get the mail. He was winded at the mailbox because of years of body neglect. He returned to the house, and sat back down on the couch. But this time, Bob didn't light up.

The next day after work, instead of his normal routine of smoking and watching TV, he walked to the end of the street. Once again,

he returned home winded, but for the second day in row, no cigarette.

On day three, Bob went around the block. Each day, Bob would push himself to go further than the day before. **He was reconnecting with his Grit.**

Within a few months, Bob ran his first 5K race. He recounts it as a horrible experience, but he finished and was hooked on running. Running races are wonderful examples of Grit, because they prove a point: **as long as you can keep putting one foot in front of the other, you can reach the finish line.**

Over 100 pounds lighter and a decade later, Bob is now an extreme distance runner, running races that last two days and cover over 100 miles —equal to four marathons. No amount of training can fully prepare the body for these types of races, and nobody finishes feeling on top of the world—but people finish these races anyway. If you finish a race like that, you have Grit. Today, Bob has completed over a dozen of these, on top of countless 5K, 10K, and half-marathon races.

Find Your Grit and Live It Everyday

Just like Bob, you need to reach down deep to find meaningful reasons for you to develop the Grit to stay in the fight. Your reason could be to reach your potential, or to prove someone wrong—or it might be the strongest and most compelling reason of all: the Grit to stay alive.

In order for Grit to yield benefits, it has to be authentic, and connected to your goals and dreams. **Which means it's not just something you do between 9 and 5—but a way of life.** Don't toy with your Grit; embrace it. It's a code for working, managing, parenting, coaching, playing and accumulating—and it will never let you down.

It's not just a smart business strategy—it could save the life of your business or you, period. It's not a matter of what you risk by being Gritty; it's what you risk by *not*. Without Grit, you're not safe. You're anything but.

Stay Gritty.

ABOUT MATT MANERO

Matt Manero combines his business brilliance with more than 20 years of hands-on experience in transportation equipment finance. Today, he is a CEO leading four companies that generate over $100,000,000 per year in business with a base of more than 10,000 clients.

Matt launched his first business, Commercial Fleet Financing, Inc., in 1995 with a phone, a folding table and the unyielding confidence of a single client, a trucker. Fast forward 20 years: Commercial Fleet Financing, Inc. made Inc. magazine's Top 500/5000 list of fastest growing companies in America in 2014. Matt is the creator and personality behind CFFnation.com, the first and only online video network featuring original programming for and by innovators, operators, movers and shakers of the transportation industry.

His companies have been recognized in trade publications such as *Overdrive, Transport Topics, Commercial Carrier Journal, and Dealer Solutions Magazine.* Matt hosts his own weekly Radio Show aptly named, "The Grit" which airs on lifestyletalkradio.com and also on CFFnation.com. In addition to *"The Grit,"* Matt has

authored a series of quick read books entitled *"10 Tips Every Trucker, Tower, Mover and Construction Co. Need to Know NOW"*, and also a forthcoming book, *"I NEED MORE MONEY,"* which reflects his battle to build his business and guides readers in creating their own future and financial success.

Reach Matt at his offices in Dallas, TX at 972.247.8447 ext 15, via email at mmanero@cffnationwide.com and on twitter @mattmanero. Learn more at cffnationwide.com and cffnation.com.